HOLT, RINEHART AND WINSTON   NEW YORK

GHOSTS
A TIME REMEMBERED

PHILIP MAKANNA

Published by Holt, Rinehart and Winston,
383 Madison Avenue, New York, New York 10017.

Published simultaneously in Canada by
Holt, Rinehart and Winston of Canada, Limited.

Library of Congress Cataloging in Publication Data

Makanna, Philip, 1940–
    Ghosts: a time remembered.

    "Fundamentals of air fighting": p.
    1. Confederate Air Force.   I. United States.
Army Air Forces. Flying Training Command.
Fundamentals of air fighting. 1979.   II. Title.
UG622.C663M34   623.74'6042'06273   79-2353
ISBN Hardbound: 0-03-047711-5
ISBN Paperback: 0-03-047716-6

First Edition

Printed in the United States of America

10 9 8 7 6 5 4 3 2 1

TO MY FATHER AND TO MY DAUGHTER:

FOR HIS COURAGE AND HIS CHALLENGE,

AND WITH THE HOPE THAT HER DREAMS WILL ALWAYS BE AS WONDERFUL AS THEY ARE TODAY.

MY SPECIAL THANKS TO COLONEL LLOYD P. NOLEN
AND COLONEL LEFTY GARDNER.

THIS BOOK WOULD NOT EXIST HAD IT NOT BEEN FOR THE WARMTH OF THE MEN AND THE WOMEN
OF THE CONFEDERATE AIR FORCE, AND THE WISDOM AND ENCOURAGEMENT OF MARION WHEELER.

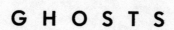

GHOSTS

I was born in 1940. I have the shadowed memory of a great rumbling sound. The screen door is banging and my mother is running across the lawn. "Planes . . ." Shading her eyes and searching the sky, she is lost in the thunder that is rolling closer. She points, and I see tiny shadows on the clouds. Fighter planes are being moved to a place beyond my imagination.

Until recently, I was never closer to the planes than I was on that afternoon, but I believed, as did most of the other little boys of my generation, that the planes were magic; we dreamed and listened to stories about them with wonder. I remember hearing that at dawn on D day, the sky was filled from horizon to horizon with black and white invasion stripes that were painted on the wings and fuselages of every plane. They were the simple, secret markings for the swarm of allied air forces that darkened the sky over the channel that day. We didn't see them, but we dreamed.

We dreamed of being test pilots and we studied silhouettes and filed blunt white-pine wings with little sandpaper paddles to make them sharp and graceful. We hung die-cast propellers on straight pins. The tiny props turned in the wind as we walked across the lawn, holding the plane overhead so it banked majestically against the sky. We saw ourselves diving out of the sun and ducking through clouds and rolling in the sky like lazy sharks. These dreams of freedom encouraged our earthbound spirits.

The generation of men who flew in that war were our fathers. They flew through a nightmare that has become a dream. Today, as retired "snowbirds" in flight from the cold midwestern winter, they wander south in campers and RVs to the farthest tip of Texas and walk alone between rows of old planes. They have tears in their eyes. What they have seen and what they see now is a mystery I can never know.

Near the point where Texas and Mexico and the Gulf come together is an air base built in 1941. It was then the site of the Harlingen Aerial Gunnery School. Hundreds of acres of concrete apron are still there, as are the huge arched hangars that were shops for the repair of hundreds of trainers and fighters and bombers. There are rows of palm trees that rustled then as they do now in the Gulf wind. There are ghosts there. I have heard them whispering near my shoulders at night as I crouched under the wings of old hospital planes that are parked out of the way, never to fly again. I have felt them over my head fluttering like moths in a steamy dawn. I have seen their shapes flickering through the blue

TV light over a lonely man on a steel bunk in the Bachelor Officers' Quarters.

He was here thirty-five years ago, during the war, when there were hundreds of people moving at every hour of the day. There were jeeps and six-bis and tank trucks running up and down the roads. The flight line had 400 T-6s moving in and out and crews and pilots for each one. Near the hangar was a bakery and a huge mess hall. The shops were active twenty-four hours of every day. P-39s were landing as rows of B-24s stood waiting for takeoff. Men left Harlingen and went to fields all over the world and flew terrifying missions. Some came back with holes in their planes. Some didn't come back, and others lay dead or dying on runways thousands of miles from south Texas.

In 1968 the Harlingen Aerial Gunnery School became Rebel Field, headquarters of the "Ghost Squadron" of the Confederate Air Force.

I first encountered the Confederate Air Force in September 1976 in Reno during an airshow that featured a reenactment of the Japanese attack on Pearl Harbor. From their base in Galveston, the Gulf Coast Wing of the Confederate Air Force had flown a B-17, a P-40, a P-39, and a half-dozen replica Zeros that Twentieth Century-Fox had made for the film *Tora! Tora! Tora!*

Soft Hawaiian music sighed over the desert as the Zeros approached in a tight formation. "December 7, 1941 . . . the time is 7:55 A.M. It is a peaceful Sunday morning near Honolulu . . ." and then balls of fire bloomed in the Nevada sand and the B-17 streamed smoke and approached a landing with only one wheel down. The P-40 and the P-39 took off to scramble with the Zeros and defend the bomber.

In a very simple form, that is what happened, but my memory of it is filled with unforgettable images among fragments of history. Pearl-gray airplanes scraped the sagebrush with rising suns as the Imperial Japanese Navy, thirty-five years out of time and place, arranged balls of red flame in a landscape of browns and dusty greens. More than 2,000 American lives had been lost at Pearl Harbor in 1941 and yet, three decades later, Japanese fighter planes, the symbolic specters of the enemy of the past, flew in formation over Nevada. This time the pilots were Texans. Among them was a rancher, a pipe fitter, a crop duster, a NASA engineer. On his forehead each wore a white bandanna centered with a rising sun and the Japanese characters that signify the "Divine Wind."

In 1281 Kublai Khan sent a huge fleet across the sea to invade

Japan. His success was almost ensured, when a wind sent by God destroyed the Chinese fleet. In 1945, young Japanese pilots wore the Rising Sun and sacrificed their lives in the belief that the Divine Wind, the kamikaze, would deliver their homeland again. Thirty-one years later the Rising Sun was being worn by Texans flying over a Nevada desert decorated with fire.

In the spring of 1977, haunted by what I had seen in Reno, I drove to Harlingen in south Texas to spend time at Rebel Field. As I started out, I told myself I was going to Texas to document the activities of a group of aviators. But I was to learn in the months that followed that I had gone because of my childhood dreams and the dreams of the generation of men that had inspired them.

On the way, I stopped in Dallas and visited one of the legendary pioneers of aviation in the Southwest. He showed me a worn brass card that identified him as a member of the International Order of Quiet Birdmen, an organization that dates back to the First World War.

"We are the Order of the Kiwi and the Modoc," he said. "The kiwi is, of course, a nonflying bird. The Modoc . . . well, you'll have to find out about that."

After this cryptic disclosure, he put his feet up on his desk and looked at the ceiling and told me about the old days, about adventure and heroism. In those moments his eyes were wet and glistening. He said he was afraid that the old spirit would die with the men who had created it. "You'll meet men in south Texas who have that spirit and that courage. Ask them about the kiwi and the Modoc."

II ✈ Lloyd P. Nolen, who invented the Confederate Air Force more than twenty years ago, first learned to fly in Denton, Texas, when he was fifteen years old.

"We had an old airplane," he told me, "a Cabin-Waco. It carried four passengers. In the springtime we'd fly out to east Texas and find a country town and buzz around it. People in those days knew that when they saw an airplane flying in circles it was probably trying to land and they'd drive out to see it. We'd have found a pasture out there someplace to land in and made arrangements to pay the farmer ten dollars for the use of the pasture all day long. When the people came out we'd take 'em for rides at all kinds of prices. That was barnstorming."

When the war started Nolen joined the Army Air Corps. At eighteen, he had already logged 300 hours of flying time so the Air Corps Training Command grabbed him, put him on inactive status, and gave him the job they needed most to fill—flight instructor.

He taught flying at civilian flying schools until the end of the war. He taught glider pilots how to fly in powered airplanes on a grass patch before they went to glider school. He taught field artillery officers how to fly Piper Cubs that they called "Maytag Messerschmitts." He was transferred to a new pasture in Terrell, Texas, to train British cadets to fly Stearmans and AT-6s. He became known as a genius in a T-6. Although he was constantly tormented by news from former students who were flying exotic planes in romantic places, he never left the United States and he never saw combat.

When the war ended, Nolen got out of the training business and into the crop-dusting business and bought a plane and headed south to the semitropical Rio Grande Valley. He made arrangements with the owners of a little country airport in Mercedes, and has been flying out of there ever since.

Mercedes is a very small town and the duster strip is miles from anything. There are no traffic corridors or safety hazards; instead, there is the freedom of a limitless sky. A pilot can go up any day and do loops and rolls and figure eights right over the hangars, or maybe wander out over the beach and run up and down the surf. No one files a flight plan when he leaves the Mercedes strip and no one worries much about what to do after he leaves the ground.

In 1951 Nolen bought a surplus P-40 Warhawk for $1,500 and his weekend exercises got more interesting. A half-dozen of his friends took turns flying the old Warhawk around the hangars of what had come to be known as (the first) Rebel Field. The most popular type of flying around Mercedes was "beating up the field." This is a British expression describing a low-level surprise attack made at very high speed. In south Texas "beating up the field" was—and is—a sport witnessed by the wise from a prone position. On a Sunday the educated spectator skitters from hangar to bush as enthusiastic pilots endeavor to keep the grasses trimmed.

Nolen sold the P-40 in 1952 to buy a faster and more powerful P-51 Mustang. The gas tank of a Mustang could be removed from the fuselage and replaced with a passenger seat. That was bound to double the fun. The Korean conflict had begun and, as it turned out, the Air Force recalled all of the surplus Mustangs and repurchased most of those that were in civilian hands. It was five years before a P-51 was available. In 1957 Nolen once again located a Mustang in El Paso. It had a chewed-up tailpiece as the result of an altercation with a light plane, but it was repairable and Nolen flew it home. The $2,500 price tag was split among Nolen and four neighbors.

The five partners rolled the airplane out one fine Sunday and found that someone had stolen into the hangar by the light of the moon and painted CONFEDERATE AIR FORCE on the fuselage below the tail. The consensus was that it sounded good, and the name stuck. Nolen and his fellow pilots started saluting one another. Then two of them commissioned each other Colonel, and the other three declared themselves Sergeants. After hamming it up for a while, the Sergeants decided that since they all owned the airplane equally, they damn well should be Colonels, too. Therefore, it was decreed on that day that "everyone in this air force is a Colonel," and that stuck, too. Today, the Confederate Air Force has eighty-three aircraft and a membership of more than 3,600 Colonels.

The Colonels realized that they couldn't dogfight with one airplane, so they started looking for another World War II airplane. The logical mate for a Mustang was a Bearcat, a Grumman F8F, which during its service career held the record for rate of climb and was the fastest and most powerful prop-driven fighter the Navy flew.

Lefty Gardner, a major personality in the CAF and Lloyd Nolen's next-door neighbor, reminisced about Nolen's second acquisition, in 1959—a year before Gardner met him—as we sipped his wife Sharon's enlightening beet wine one night to the tune of sugarcane trucks howling past the Mercedes airstrip.

"One day the Navy called up and said, 'You want your Bearcats, Double-L P?' Lloyd said, 'What Bearcats?' The Navy said, 'The two you bid eight hundred and five dollars for. You won them. If you want them, get yourself out to Litchfield Park in Arizona and fly them out of here.'

"So Lloyd went to Phoenix and spent all day long looking over thirty-two Bearcats that were filled with red sand and had been sitting in hundred-and-ten-degree heat for ten years. The commander of the base said, 'Get one of those airplanes out of here today because we're fixin' to close this space and melt those Bearcats down.' About four fifty-nine the commander walked back out and said, 'When are you fixin' to leave with your Bearcat?' Lloyd told him, 'Well, I'm fixin' to leave just as soon as I can figure out how to get in it and crank it up.' The commander said, 'Well, you push that button right there and you can open the canopy and get in. Then punch that shiny button right there and fire it up and *leave* here! Now, when you leave, don't you ever come back!' So Lloyd said, 'Okay. Adios,' and the commander turned on his heel and left.

"Lloyd pushed all the shiny buttons and the plane fired up and he taxied out to the end of the runway. He proceeded to take off, and pushed another button and the gear came up. He got up about two thousand feet and the engine quit. He probably was figuring to himself, 'I expect I ought to go back and land at the base 'cause it's a little smoother back there than it is out here.' So he did a hundred-and-eighty-degree turn and lit back to the base and the commander came roarin' out and said, 'I thought I told you not to come back to this base once you left here.' Lloyd said, 'Well, Commander, I thought I could negotiate with you better than I could with those sand dunes, so I came back.'

"The base commander said, 'Well, okay. Here are some new spark plugs. You put 'em in right now and depart again.' About three days, forty-eight plugs, several mechanics, and mucho cerveza later, Lloyd took off and headed for El Paso."

As Lefty tells it, it took three weeks and further romantic aeronautical incidents in 100-degree heat before Nolen and his Bearcat arrived home at Rebel Field, Mercedes. The second Bearcat was retrieved a few weeks later. The remaining F8Fs were dragged to the smelter and destroyed.

The Confederate Air Force now had three airplanes and five Colonels. When officers of the Naval Air Station at Kingsville asked them to demonstrate the Mustang and the Bearcat at their airshow in 1960, they were genuinely surprised. The CAF Colonels thought the new jets were the glamorous way to fly, but they soon learned that they weren't glamorous to those who flew them. The early jets were underpowered. They had huge appetites for fuel and limited capacities for carrying it. This made predetermined flight plans a necessity. The freedom and enjoyment of flying began to belong to the past. After the airshow Navy pilots came out to the flight line at sunset, crawled up inside the old warbirds, and sat dreaming of flying the huge four-blade propellers . . . of boring holes in the clouds. It was a dream that was hard to forget.

Lefty Gardner was in his early twenties during the war. He flew forty-three missions—thirteen of them as "tail-end Charlie"—piloting a B-17 over Germany. In 1950 Gardner originated airborne brush control in west Texas and became something of a legendary character as the cowboy aviator. "Flyin' mesquite," as Gardner termed his version of crop-dusting, required dramatic aerial flip-flops over the vast areas of range that make up the Panhandle ranches. To achieve greater maneuverability, he customized his Stearman biplanes with special high-lift wings that allowed them to drift down the sides of cliffs and climb out of canyons hanging on the propeller.

Lefty Gardner met Lloyd Nolen in 1960. Gardner was living up north of Laredo and was in the market for radial motors for his Stearmans. They were very scarce at the time but he located several and to check on them called Nolen, who suggested that he forget about the ones he had found and instead, fly with him to Canada "to get the same engines with airplanes attached." Lloyd Nolen had a sharp eye for the makings of a Colonel and the Confederate Air Force began the induction of Lefty Gardner.

"The next thing I knew," Gardner remembers, "Lloyd was flying up to Crystal City through lightning and thunderclouds blacker'n the inside of a cow. Of course, I should have known that there was something fishy about a guy who would fly through weather like that just to pick me up to take me to Canada to get a good deal on a couple of engines. When Lloyd came, he brought all the pilots he had, so I rounded up all the pilots I had and we flew to Canada. We landed at Lethbridge, Alberta, at an abandoned air base and when we flung open the door of the hangar there was a bunch of T-6s scattered all over the floor. They didn't have engines on 'em or radios in 'em. They didn't even have wings on 'em. But, I knew that we had found some low-time airplanes and if we could get 'em back to Texas we'd be able to fly the heck out of 'em—and then sell 'em for a fortune."

"For two or three days we talked to a lawyer and Lloyd talked to me about the Confederate Air Force. He told me about the thrill of flying a Mustang and a Bearcat and about how much more fun those fighters were to fly than a Stearman or a bomber—all that kind of stuff.

"We finally got our T-6s put together and spun 'em back to Texas and Lloyd put me in the back seat of the Mustang and flew me around the hangars and showed me the Bearcat, which, according to him, is a much better plane than the Mustang. My blood pressure was one ninety-five over seventy and I was ready to go. So he said, 'I happen to know that there's a Corsair out in Buckeye, Arizona. Why don't you go get it?'"

Thus began a tradition of quests. In years to come, rusty derelicts were located in swamps and snowbanks all over North and South America and Europe. They were flown, often at great risk, to south Texas. There they were restored and the Confederate Air Force grew.

In the spring of 1962 the mythical Colonel Jethro E. Culpeper, phantom Commander of the CAF, whose directives are conveyed by his Deputy Commander, Colonel Nolen, awarded Colonel Gardner the Silver Magnolia Blossom (Heroic) for the recovery of the CAF's first P-38. Lefty and his brother, Colonel Henry Gardner, had flown to Hayward, California, to retrieve a Hellcat. Lefty had acquired the P-38 in the process. The citation describing the task and skills that distinguished the new Colonel (formerly an innocent little ole crop duster from Crystal City, Texas) reads in part:

. . . Lefty Gardner, 60-110, Colonel, Confederate Air Force, for gallantry in action in the heroic achievement and at great personal risk, in connection with military operations over Yankee strongholds in the vicinity of California, Arizona, and Florida, did, under extremely adverse conditions, achieve the following:

Early on the morning of 10 September 1961, weary-eyed from poisonous Yankee whiskey and from thwarting off a nightlong attack and harassment by a damyankee spy, Col. Gardner managed to find his way to the Sacramento Airport to take delivery of one P-38 aircraft on behalf of the Confederate Air Force and deliver said aircraft to CAF Headquarters, Rebel Field, Texas. Upon completion of the transaction and acceptance, Col. Gardner discovered that all maintenance manuals, pilot's manuals, and operations instructions had been stolen by Yankee spies. This would have been a devastating blow to a lesser man; however, Col. Gardner immediately deduced that since this aircraft had two engines and two tails, he simply would do everything as in other aircraft except he would do it two times. Col. Gardner seated himself in this great flying machine, surveyed the cockpit, and determined the use and purpose of each and every lever and switch—except four—stowed his gear in proper place, started the engines, roared down the runway and into the blue of the California sky and headed for DIXIE. . . .

. . . While crossing the Sierra Mountains, Col. Gardner found that his main fuel tank had become filled with air. At this point, the engines pulled a typical Yankee trick—they quit. With utmost dispatch and cool logic and calm determination, Col. Gardner moved all switches and valves until the engines again began to function. Having surmounted these difficulties he was then, through exceptional skill in the science of navigation, able to locate the State of Arizona. . . .

As he moved across the Texas border, a strong Texas tailwind began to impede his progress to the degree that even though his indicated airspeed was 272 mph it took him 1:82 minutes to fly from El Paso to Midland, a distance of 250 miles. After landing and gassing at Midland, Col. Gardner, due to his superior intelligence and skillful airmanship, calculated that the cause of his low ground speed was the fact that this strong tailwind had blown his flaps down. With this successfully corrected, he sailed into Rebel Field, undaunted by the fact that his wife shook her fist at him as he passed over his home at Crystal City, his having been gone only one week and nine days on a three-day trip.

This being his third and least hazardous ferrying experience with the Confederate Air Force, having previously brought an FG1D Corsair from the dust of Arizona and a P-40 Warhawk from the swamps of Florida, Col. Gardner was not in the least shook-up by these mild and minor miscalculations. The CIA (Confederate Intelligence Agency) has classified the Florida and Arizona flights TOP SECRET. It can be revealed, however, that in the case of the P-40, Col. Gardner ascertained that saboteurs had stolen the pitch out of his prop and the cob out of his carburetor and the gin out of his generator. In the case of the Corsair, it was obvious that someone had put the wings on upside down. . . .

. . . His actions will do much to familiarize this and coming generations with these great fighting aircraft as well as with the superior military judgment, tactical skill, and tremendous personal courage of this great Rebel. The high qualities of judgment, courage, and devotion to duty displayed by Col. Gardner, and the fact that he got here a-tall, reflects great credit upon himself and the Confederate Air Force.

By 1963 the CAF had acquired one example of each of the ten American fighter planes from World War II: a North American P-51 Mustang, a Republic P-47 Thunderbolt, a Chance Vought FG1D Corsair, a Curtiss P-40 Warhawk, a Grumman F4F Wildcat (General Motors FM-2), a Lockheed P-38 Lightning, a Bell P-39 Airacobra, a Grumman F8F Bearcat, a Grumman F6F Hellcat, and a Bell P-63 Kingcobra.

The Colonels then began looking for World War II American bombers. They found a B-25 Mitchell, a medium bomber, and an A-26 Invader, an attack bomber and night fighter, and flew them successfully from the strip at Mercedes. A Douglas A-20 Havoc, a twin-engined light bomber, was tracked down, and, in 1967, a Martin B-26 medium bomber was located in Denver.

The activity in the air on Sundays in Mercedes was becoming famous, and Rebel Field could not comfortably accommodate the tremendous crowds that the airshows attracted. Parked cars and pickup trucks slowed traffic for miles around the duster strip. The Colonels were beginning to talk about expanding their collection to include the "heavies"—maybe a B-17 Flying Fortress or a B-24 Liberator—but the 2,900-foot runway at Mercedes was too short and had too light a base to support a heavy bomber.

In 1968 the city of Harlingen offered the CAF a new home at the former Harlingen Aerial Gunnery School. The Colonels moved their headquarters fourteen miles east and christened the World War II air base Rebel Field. Mercedes became Old Rebel Field.

Shortly thereafter the CAF took delivery of a B-17 and a B-24 that had been in service for Petróleos Mexicano, the Mexican national oil company. The big bombers had been resident at Lefty Gardner's base in Brownwood, Texas. Brownwood city officials, in concert with Lefty, had decided that they were less than desirable. Negotiations for a Spitfire began. Messerschmitts were found in Spain. In 1970 a B-29 was located in the California desert, where it had been standing since 1954 and was now scheduled to be a standing target for ballistic missile tests. A pilot, flying over the China Lake Ordnance Depot, spotted the huge silver silhouette—a fugitive from naval rockets. A crew of CAF mechanics and pilots headed by Lefty Gardner was soon deployed and spent nine weeks in the desert working on the Superfortress. On August 3, 1971—for the first time in seventeen years—the old bomber slowly lifted itself from the floor of the Mojave Desert. It flew nonstop to Harlingen in six hours and thirty-eight minutes.

Near Ontario, California, the Colonels located a Curtiss SB2C Helldiver, the ponderous "Big-tailed Beast" that had been the standard carrier-based dive bomber at the end of the war. It stood on rotting tires, at the end of a runway in Chino. Every window in its canopy was broken and pigeons had been roosting in the cockpits for ten years. A detachment of bats hung in the gloom behind the tail gunner's harness and, farther down, the shadows had spawned the largest colony of black widow spiders north of Acapulco. Colonel Bob Griffin became sponsor of the SB2C and dispatched two Confederate mechanics to the Coast with a truck and a trailer to restore it and fly it home. One year later, piloted by Colonel Gerald Martin, the "Beast" flew back to Texas, becoming the only flyable Helldiver of the 6,000 that were built.

In 1971, Colonel Ed Jurist bought a DeHavilland Mosquito in England. Prized by the Royal Air Force pilots for its versatility, the "Mossie" flew higher and faster than most other World War II fighters. This was largely due to the fact that, except for its two Rolls-Royce engines, it was made of plywood. In December of 1971, Colonels Jurist and Duane Egli flew the Mosquito from London to the Azores and then across the North Atlantic to Newfoundland. In London Colonel Egli had replaced camshafts in both engines, overhauled both carburetors, overhauled four magnetos, and removed a bird's nest from the right main fuel cell. Navigation and communications radios had failed over the coast of Spain in a shower of sparks and the "Mossie" had scattered most of its exhaust stacks across the Atlantic. On the second of January, 1972, they landed the thirty-one-year-old plywood frame at Rebel Field, climaxing an extraordinary period of CAF aircraft recovery. The Confederate Air Force now consisted of fifty-six aircraft (see page 23).

The maintenance of the Confederate Air Force aircraft is an enormous task. Most of the airplanes are more then thirty years old and the FAA regularly inspects each aircraft to ensure that all are maintained to standards. The annual inspection of the B-29 requires 288 hours of labor—nine days for a crew of four. Fifty miles of tubing and cable are checked, as are the 342 functions of the landing gear and the hydraulic and electrical systems. One hundred and five functions are checked in each of the four engines, and 144 spark plugs and 340 gallons of oil are changed.

The CAF maintains the only Helldiver, Dauntless, and F-82 Twin Mustang that still fly. Many parts are now unavailable. Confederate Air Force hangars are filled with crates of exotic bits and pieces that solve a lot of problems, but piece by piece, the extensive stock of equipment manufactured in the forties is disappearing. Each part has a finite life and when a piston burns, a cam wears flat, or a cylinder head cracks, there is no replacement at hand. New parts must be specially built or custom-made to fit the requirement.

The CAF's mechanical ingenuity was a demonstrable reality one wet summer morning in 1977 in Harlingen. The FAA had grounded the F-82 Twin Mustang immediately after it landed at Rebel Field in 1969. To get it flying again, a complicated rebuild was necessary. Of late, the task had become the pet project of Colonel Malcolm Russell, one of the geniuses of the CAF's staff of mechanics. After many months of creative tinkering, Russell had gotten the Rolls-Royce Merlin V-12 engines in running order and had solved a critical mechanical problem by adapting the brake drums from another airplane to the Twin Mustang's system.

It was a special morning for Colonel Russell. When the rain stopped at eight-thirty, he carefully towed the big twin-engined fighter from its hangar, pulled each prop to a precisely vertical position, fussed in the cockpit for a minute, and then, finding himself alone in the little yellow tug, he raced out across the concrete apron dodging and splashing through puddles that had formed in the dawn rain. Colonel Gardner climbed into the cockpit about nine-thirty. The mechanics assembled on the wing for a conference and then everybody moved back. Gardner pushed buttons, the Merlins coughed smoke, fire ballooned out of the stacks, and both engines caught. Russell moved close behind the huge spinning blades and leaned on the prop wash. Holding a tubular frame member, he pulled himself off his feet, and reached up and put the flat of his hand into the exhaust as it came out of each of the twenty-four stacks. Because of the terrible roar of the engines the best way to tell if every cylinder is firing is to feel the heat of each exhaust. Gardner revved a motor—blue fire smacked Russell's palm and the prop wash nearly blew him into the wing. Gardner shut the motors down and Colonel Russell's feet came back to earth.

He climbed onto the wing to confer with Gardner. He was grinning. Thumbs up. The little flags of hair that remain on the sides of his head were standing back like Mercury's wings. It had been a critical and successful test session.

III ✈ When I arrived in Harlingen in May 1977, I checked into a motel on the Sunshine Strip and waited for a few days to hear from Colonel Lloyd Nolen. I had already spoken to Colonel Nolen, who had been introduced to me as the Colonel in Charge of Literary Affairs, about the book I hoped to put together on the Confederate Air Force. Finally Nolen agreed to meet me and invited me to join him for dinner. When he arrived at the door of my motel room, Nolen first encountered my dog, Pal, a friendly terrier of various breeding. He studied Pal for a long and serious moment, and then he spoke as much to himself as to me, "A guy with a dog like that couldn't be all bad."

After he stepped inside Colonel Nolen addressed a few polite words to me and then regarded Pal for a long stretch. We both fidgeted a little. Colonel Nolen was concerned about the sincerity of the stranger who stood before him with the smiling dog. Pal's wisdom was apparent, but the project proposed by his master was not to be taken lightly and there was always the possibility that the dog was just a front.

His next words were, "Offhand, I'd say he's a trick dog."

Fortunately he said this with warmth and the awkwardness between us vanished. Pal is now an unofficial Colonel in the Confederate Air Force. His photograph hangs in the headquarters building at Rebel Field. I have no doubt that it was because of him that I was invited to fly in a number of extraordinary airplanes, piloted by some very extraordinary men.

They say John Huston keeps a dumb old horse in his barn for the initiation of strangers, and that when anyone but Huston climbs aboard, the dumb old horse becomes a dragon. A wise man will say, "Thank you, Mr. Huston, but I think I won't ride that dumb old horse today."

I flew with Colonel Lefty Gardner in his Mustang for half an hour one afternoon when I was still a newcomer to the Confederate Air Force. I should have remembered the story about Huston's horse. We went down the dusty Mercedes strip and I felt the gear come in just a few feet off the ground. Next thing I knew, we were pointed straight up and the the right wing was straight down. Then the whole damn thing was pointing straight down and we buzzed Old Rebel Field below the roof of the hangar. After that, distinct memory escapes me. I remember going straight up into the blue sky and thin clouds. We rolled at the top of that loop and I saw the earth swing in over my head, but there was no sense of falling; not a sharp or jarring movement. The Mustang gained altitude and we bored graceful holes in the clouds.

Then Lefty decided to come in low around the side of the hangar with a wing in the grass. We were upside down at least once and sideways a lot. He said he was scouting for rattlesnakes. He did a few eight-point rolls and banged the wings precisely to their stops like a snappy British salute. From time to time, he stretched around and peeked at me with one eye. I was told later that he has dropped the landing gear of his P-38 in the middle of a roll when he was only a few feet off the ramp. He has made rooster tails with his wheels in the Rio Grande. I figure I got off easy. Next time out, I decided I would ride on my back so I could see the ground.

We landed. Grinning faces came out of hiding places behind bushes and confused cows. Old Bob Maxwell, who flew a bomber over Germany on his eighteenth birthday, climbed out on the wing of the Mustang with a fuel hose, mumbling and laughing to himself after hearing Lefty's landing request: "We'll take seventy-five gallons, sir. And just charge that to the Army."

I flew in a B-17, a BT-13, an AT-6, a replica Kate torpedo bomber, a T-34, a Douglas Dauntless, a Curtiss Helldiver, two Mustangs, and a Stearman rigged to fly under barbed-wire fences. These flights originated from grass patches, deserted air bases, commercial airports, and nearly everything in between.

Sounds I heard in my first days in south Texas will be in my ears forever: the smooth, whistling bellow of the twin Allison V-12s in a P-38, the nasty rap from the short exhaust stacks of the Mustangs, the deep boom of the big Navy radials. I slept to the howls and rattles of a rusty air-conditioner that drew the Gulf wind in and left it damp and clammy.

I used two 35mm. Nikon F-2 cameras with 20mm., 85mm., 200mm., and 500mm. Nikkor lenses. I learned that the best way to deal with the huge space of the various airfields was to spread out all of my equipment in the trunk of the car between the folds of a bunched-up blanket and drive from shot to shot. I am absolutely in love with flying but must admit that flying upside down with the

Colonels is hard on my stomach. Of course this only encourages the Colonel who is doing the flips. I felt poorly on more than one occasion and always tried to smile when they glanced over their shoulders at me.

The U.S. Air Force invited the Confederate Air Force to participate in an airshow at the Selfridge Air National Guard base near Detroit on July 4, 1977, to celebrate the sixtieth anniversary of the base, which was the military's first training field.

I joined the veteran Colonels as guests of the new generation of airmen. Colonel Ed Messick, Operations Officer, held his usual rowdy but efficient briefing before the airshow. He wore the official gray Confederate hat and carried a softball bat for a swagger stick. The young Air Force pilots were crowded into the rear of the briefing room and watched in silent amazement while Colonel Messick was cheered and booed as he defined the coming day's events.

In the middle of the briefing, Colonel Jim Hill, who, as a member of the American Volunteer Group in the late thirties, flew a "gooney bird over the hump" (a C–47 transport over the Himalayas) into China, rose slowly and began to mutter something about getting out to his airplane. "They're coming. . . . They're coming. . . . Get me to the flight line. . . ." Then the beloved, craggy Colonel turned, slumped, and fell over the row of seats in front of him. His head was down. He was coughing and holding his chest as he sagged to the floor. For a moment his feet were up in the air. He came down like a wet towel.

Messick called for oxygen. Then, still clutching his softball bat, he collapsed on the floor too. CAF doctors jumped up and rushed to Hill's side. His cracked, veined hands trembled as they rose and fell behind the seat backs several times. Members of the CAF pulled him from between the seats. The young U.S. airmen arrived with oxygen. The room was silent and frozen to the moment.

Messick was standing again. He had a can of beer in his hand. He popped it, sprinkled some on Colonel Hill, and pronounced, "He'll be all right. He just needs his beer and his airplane!"

At this, Jim Hill was on his feet. He clapped his hands over his head, hopped around, and proclaimed his victory. The assembled Colonels cheered. The young Air Force men wobbled to the back of the hall, Messick straightened his Stetson, raised the softball bat, and sent us out into the sunshine.

The Colonels had performed a macabre ritual to exorcise fear.

The young pilots who left the windowless room rigid and amazed seemed relieved that the briefing was over.

In early September I flew to El Paso to meet Colonel Messick to fly with him to Phoenix for the CAF's Labor Day Airshow. At the briefing in El Paso, Messick scheduled all of the takeoffs so that the participating CAF aircraft would meet over Phoenix at the same time. The Zeros were airborne first because they had to stop for fuel at the halfway point and then, one by one, the old planes took to the air. Messick would take off last. I was to be his passenger.

Messick's P-51 is a trick model with auxiliary fuel cells in the wing that allow him to stay in the air for eight hours. The canopy is tinted. The cockpit is customized and plush. Any sharp edge is covered with leather and both seats are upholstered in tuck-and-roll red flannel. I almost expected a walnut bar to pop out of the floor.

I polished the canopy to clear the view for my camera and shoved a half-dozen antistatic wipers into the map pocket for future polishing. I expected that I might get fingerprints inside the bubble as we flew and I wanted to be prepared to clean them off. I stuffed my cameras and then myself into the rear seat. I put on the shoulder harness and a seatbelt and was enveloped by the leather all around

me. The back seat of a Mustang is no place for someone who likes to get out of airplanes fast. I couldn't move, hear, or breathe.

I observed Colonel Messick, as he was described in his Citation for the Order of the Brass Jackass, pull on his "helmet, goggles, push-button watch, buckle-over shoes, silk scarf, and leap lightly into the cockpit. Waving to the crowd in the manner of Smilin' Jack and Tailspin Tommy, he adjusted his goggles, engaged the starting lever, and the mighty Merlin roared into life."

A Mustang has a 1,500-horsepower engine, with two banks of six cylinders in line. It starts in a cloud of smoke and fire that bursts out of the little stacks and is blown back past the cockpit by a rush of air off the propeller. There is a tremendous amount of noise and vibration. A Mustang is a tail dragger and the engine housing extends so high and far in front that there is no way of seeing straight ahead when the plane is at rest on the ground.

Messick zigzagged down the length of the taxiway, looking out this side and then the other to see where he was going. We lined up next to a P-47. Messick turned up the wick. There was an explosion of noise and wind and the plane skipped into the air. In formation off our right wing, the huge P-47 Jug folded its gear and climbed fast behind us.

We flew for an hour before we sighted the bombers. I spotted a C-45 first. It was a thousand feet below us, its polished skin flashing in the New Mexico sun. Then, higher and to the north, I saw the B-17, the B-24, and then the gracefully monstrous B-29. Over the headset Messick offered to come in close for pictures. I learned that "come in close" means "come in close sideways," "come in close upside down," "come in close on the top side of a barrel roll." The upside-down photographer with one eye on the camera and the other eye searching for ground in zero gravity is an unhappy passenger. Somewhere between a whifferdill and a Beauregard flip my midriff insecurity interrupted my trigger finger. Grabbing for the antistatic wipers at the bottom of the cockpit, while wishing I had brought one of those doggie bags graciously provided by the airlines, I noticed long pieces of black fur trailing over the red carpet. I pulled myself up and, peering into the seat ahead, I discovered that my pilot had pulled a rubber monkey face over his head and was making primate gestures at the crew of the B-24.

All of the planes gathered in orbit over Phoenix International Raceway, and joined formation. Led by the Tora Tora crew—a dozen Japanese Zeros, Kates, and Val torpedo bombers—we flew low over suburban Phoenix.

It was over 120 degrees at that altitude, and because Colonel Messick was running the show and had those dandy eight-hour tanks, we were the last to land. I think I have never felt worse in my life.

The temperature on the flight line in Phoenix over the Labor Day weekend of 1977 stood at 125 degrees during the two days of the airshow. On the first day there were 350 cases of heat prostration; on the second day almost everyone carried an umbrella for protection from the sun.

First there was the national anthem. Then, for two hours, CAF aircraft took to the air to reenact scenarios from Spain in 1936, the Battle of Britain, Pearl Harbor, the North African campaign, Ploeşti, Normandy, and Hiroshima. Solo aerobatics performed by Colonel Gerald Martin in a Wildcat and by Colonel Lefty Gardner in a P-38 provided intermissions between battle sequences.

As I crossed the runway with Colonels Bill McCoy and Al Jenkins to help prepare the explosive charges that simulate bomb bursts produced for the various air battles, the heat was almost unbearable. We loaded dynamite from steel and concrete blockhouses into pickup trucks and strung wire over the desert from blasting caps to breaker boxes. We placed gray plastic pails full of gasoline on top of the explosives and topped them off with crankcase oil. It was a slow, dangerous job that demanded order and delicacy.

There was no more than a moment of rest before the Zeros appeared. They came in just a few feet off the Arizona sand and fire began boiling 100 feet into the hot air. Across the shimmering runway, a mirage of 50,000 silent people stood with black umbrellas over their heads.

Suddenly the ghosts were all around me. As the Zeros came in I was only feet away. They passed and the air writhed and shrieked and tore at itself in a turbulent aftershock. I turned and saw a P-40 painted with jaws of the Flying Tiger skim into the mirage . . . the teeth of the shark . . . the phantom mouth of death. I stood and walked through clouds of oily smoke. I was pressed by hot concussions as the fuel vaporized and boiled into the sky. I had strayed into a level of Hell. The moment was frozen and I was wandering with spirits from another time.

The events at Phoenix and at other airshows around the country are part of a ceremony created by a generation of men who saw the ritual as reality thirty-five years ago. They experienced being on the edge that defines life; they saw their friends pass over the brink and not return. They lived through the tragedy of it as only they can know it. The eternal is of no consequence to them because they are part of it. It is both reassuring and unnerving to be with them and watch them flirt with the angel of death.

Dawn is a moment that aviators consider enchanted. It provides a door to the unknown. As the sun nears the edge of the horizon there is a silent aura of magic—birds and animals pause. First light imparts a calm to the air and to those who would fly into it.

Except for the unrestored hospital planes that stand forgotten at the back of the ramp, the flight line of the old Harlingen Aerial Gunnery School is deserted at dawn most of the year. But, in October, for four mornings, men move quietly on the concrete in the darkness before the sunrise. Motors start in the gloom and the planes rise up through the mist and fly out above a lacework of green and brown to rendezvous over the Gulf. A squadron of ghosts—Avengers, Wildcats, Hellcats, Bearcats, Mustangs, Warhawks, Zeros, Thunderbolts, Lightnings, and a Helldiver, a Dauntless, a Flying Fortress, and a Liberator—fly in formation over a silent sea as the sun cracks through the darkened sky.

On one of these mornings I flew with Colonel Larry Irvine in the only surviving SBD Dauntless, the Navy's principal dive bomber in the early years of the war. The Dauntless was old when the war began. Its design dates back to a Navy contract in 1934. From the open canopy I could see the roundheaded rivets that preceded the flush rivets, protruding from the wing like navy-blue bubbles. As we drifted alone through the warm, damp air, a B-25 bomber crossed the sky overhead and then, diving down over our left wing, disappeared. A P-40, a Messerschmitt, and a Hellcat followed in flashes. They flew out of the sunrise over the Gulf toward a steaming south Texas landscape and the palm trees of the Harlingen Aerial Gunnery School.

We followed an Avenger out over the Gulf that morning. We never got very close. It remained some distance away and then disappeared into the gold reflected by the sea. We dropped low over the beach, flew for miles just a few feet off the waves, and returned to base.

On an overcast evening in Harlingen, Colonel Bob Maxwell took my arm and led me away from the hangars. We walked hundreds of yards until we were near the center of the huge concrete ramp. There was nothing out there except an occasional recess that hides the steel eyes used to tie down T-6s flown during the war. By way of explanation, Maxwell simply said that he wanted me to see "Hines's name." He pointed to the concrete near where we stood and I read "H-I-N-E-S" written in tar. Maxwell had been there when Hines had written his name on the runway in 1943. In 1945, Maxwell learned that Hines, a gunner in a B-17, had been killed somewhere in Europe. He was silent for a moment; then continued. He told me that during the war crewmen, with time on their hands as they stood alone at their positions across the vast ramp, dug the sun-softened tar from between the cracks that separated the slabs and dabbed their marks on the concrete. As we walked away slowly, I saw around me the initials "T. L.," the name "Jo," "D. J. M." with a square around it, the words "Hawaii" and "Texas." When I drew back, I could see hundreds of names and marks and symbols across the concrete. I remembered that Native Americans tapped the flat faces of cliffs with small rocks and made indelible marks and symbols, called petroglyphs, at important locations—at crossroads or where canyons narrowed. In similar fashion, it seemed to me, Hines and the other men knew that they stood at a crossing. They made their mark in a nearly indestructible medium.

It began to rain as Maxwell and I continued to talk and we

went to the far end of the ramp and took shelter under the wing of one of the hospital planes. Lightning flared all around us. I made one photograph.

I remember now as I write this what the old aviator in Dallas said about the International Order of Quiet Birdmen. "We are the Order of the Kiwi and the Modoc. The kiwi is, of course, a nonflying bird. The Modoc . . . well, you'll have to find out about that."

I had speculated that the Modoc was also a bird. I have since learned that the Modoc were a tribe of American Indians. They were warriors known for their courage and respected for their distinctive customs and unique way of life. After relinquishing most of their lands, the Modoc were resettled on a reservation. A renegade band defied the U.S. Army and fled the reservation, where they had been forced to live with other displaced Indian tribes. The Army hunted them down and, after a bloody war in 1873, hanged their leader and sent the survivors to a reservation in Oklahoma to separate them from their tribesmen forever. By the 1960s the Modoc numbered less than 1,500. Their traditions are forgotten and their spirit is the memory of only a few.

The Headquarters Wing—Harlingen, Texas

The Alamo Wing—San Antonio, Texas

The Arizona Wing—Phoenix, Arizona

The Cajun Wing—Lafayette, Louisiana

The Central Texas Wing—San Marcos, Texas

The Colorado Wing—Aurora, Colorado

The Dallas/Fort Worth Wing—Dallas, Texas

The Florida Wing—Daytona Beach, Florida

The Gulf Coast Wing—Galveston, Texas

The Mid-Atlantic Wing—Harrisburg, Pennsylvania

The New Mexico Wing—Hobbs, New Mexico

The Oklahoma Wing—Oklahoma City, Oklahoma

The Razorback Wing—Pine Bluff, Arkansas

The Southern Minnesota Wing—Minneapolis, Minnesota

The West Texas Wing—San Angelo, Texas

The Australian Squadron—Townsville, New South Wales

The New Zealand Squadron—Auckland, New Zealand

B-17 Flying Fortress

B-24 Liberator (LB-30)

B-25 Mitchell (3 each)

B-26 Marauder

A-20 Havoc

A-26 Invader (2 each)

Lockheed Hudson

B-29 Superfortress

P-38 Lightning

P-51D Mustang (2 each)

P-51C Mustang

P-39 Airacobra

P-40 Warhawk

P-47 Thunderbolt

P-63 Kingcobra

FG1D Corsair

FM2 Wildcat

F6F Hellcat

F8F Bearcat

F-82 Twin Mustang

Messerschmitt ME 109 (4 each)

Spitfire MK IX

SB2C Helldiver

DeHavilland MK 35 Mosquito

SBD Dauntless

TBM Avenger

PBY-5A Catalina

C-47 Skytrain

Messerschmitt ME 108

C-45

T-6 Texan (2 each)

BT-15 Vultee

PT-17 Stearman (2 each)

PT-22 (2 each)

PT-19

PT-26

Focke Wulf 44 Stiegletz

Stinson L-5

Replica Val (Japanese dive bomber) (2 each)

Replica Kate (Japanese torpedo bomber)

Replica Zero (Japanese fighter) (5 each)

COLOR PLATES

PLATE 1

PLATE 2

PLATE 3

PLATE 4

PLATE 5

PLATE 6

PLATE 7

PLATE 8

PLATE   9

PLATE 10

PLATE 11

PLATE 12

PLATE 13

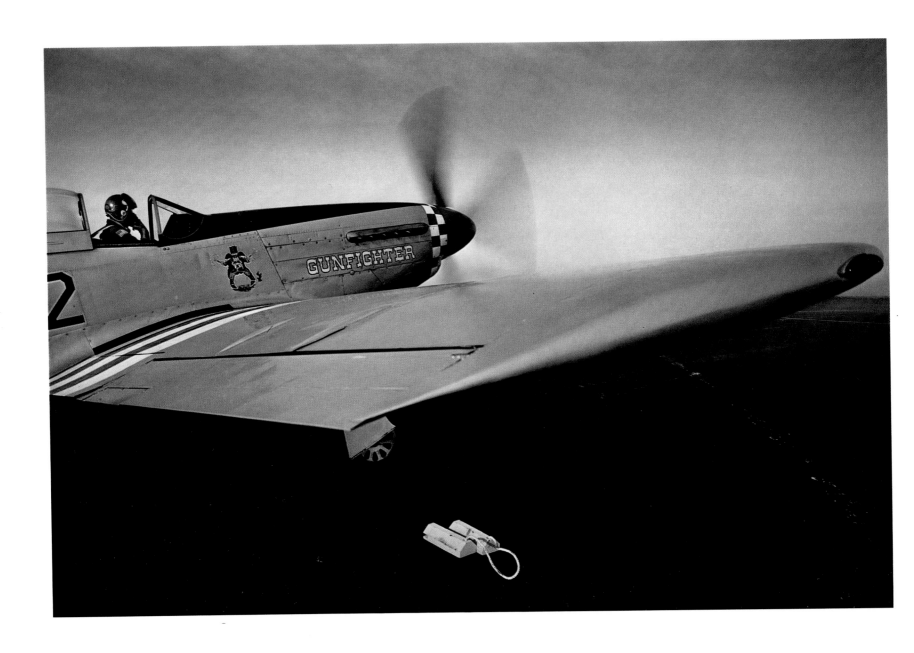

PLATE 14

PLATE 15

PLATE 16

PLATE 21

PLATE 22

PLATE 23

PLATE 24

PLATE 25

PLATE 26

PLATE 27

PLATE 28

PLATE 29

PLATE 30

PLATE   31

PLATE 32

PLATE 33

PLATE 34

PLATE 35

PLATE 36

PLATE 37

PLATE 38

PLATE 39

PLATE 40

PLATE 41

PLATE 42

PLATE 43

PLATE 44

PLATE 45

PLATE 46

PLATE 47

PLATE 48

FUNDAMENTALS OF
AIR FIGHTING

Fundamentals of Air Fighting, a restricted pamphlet issued by the Adjutant General's Office of the War Department and published by the United States Government Printing Office in 1942, was distributed to fighter and bomber pilots in the early days of World War II.*

*The fundamentals are reproduced here in their original style and format.

FOREWORD

The information contained in the following pages has been derived from official and accurate reports of actual air combats and operations. Much of what is repeated here is as old as air fighting itself. The information portrayed is disseminated not as inflexible rules or directives, but rather imparts something of what has been learned of air operations thus far and to encourage initiative and study of the subjects covered by all flying personnel. The air fighter must be constantly awake to all developments, be ever alert to use his best talents to meet the ever fast moving panorama of air warfare. To anticipate future developments one must have some knowledge of past and present methods.

I. GUNNERY PRINCIPLES

IN AIR COMBAT, the purpose of the fighter pilot, and flexible gunners, is to destroy the enemy quickly with the minimum amount of ammunition. This can best be accomplished by developing superior fire power, and firing at decisive range, which depend on:

> Accuracy of gun sighting,
> Number and type of guns and amount of
> ammunition available,
> Correct estimation of range,
> Concentration of fire power.

Concentration of fire power may be considered in two parts, viz:

Concentration of fire in time and space depending upon the number of guns that can be brought to bear either from a single aircraft or from a formation;

Bullet density built up during fire, depending on time and range.

The area of space covered by the fire from a single gun is termed the "bullet group" for that gun.

The primary consideration is to obtain a bullet density which is likely to destroy the expected target.

The *total* "lethal area" of a target is the sum of the various small vulnerable or vital areas in the target in which it is probable that one bullet would result in disabling or destroying one target aircraft.

Bullet density, and the size of the bullet group are directly proportional to range, i.e., the diameter of the group at 400 yards is four times that at 100 yards.

It is imperative, in air combat, that a lethal density be built up quickly because—

The opportunities for accurate shooting are short,
The quicker the lethal density is built up the less likely you are yourself to be shot down.

Increased lethal density can be built up by—

Higher rate of gun fire,
Increased number of guns,
Mutual support between guns of two or more aircraft,
Reduction of range,
Increased caliber of guns.

II. AIR FIGHTING PRINCIPLES

A FUNDAMENTAL of all air fighting tactics is *simplicity* and *flexibility*.

Tactics must be simple because of the *time factor*. The speed of modern aircraft does not admit of the development of elaborate formations and attacks. Other factors which demand simplicity are—

Difficulty of control,
Limited vision,

Difficulties of intercommunication,

Fleeting opportunity for decisive air combat,

Necessity of exploitation of varying weather conditions so as
to effect surprise, viz; clouds, sun, haze, dawn, and dusk
lighting effects.

Another fundamental affecting fighting tactics is MORALE and
LEADERSHIP. A high morale is essential. It is dependent upon
physical fitness, environment, a contented frame of mind and
good leadership.

The leader must possess initiative and skill to judge when
and from which direction maximum fire should be brought to
bear. He must inspire confidence in air crews and know their
ability and limitations. The good leader will aim to achieve a
decisive success with the whole force under his command
rather than to gain a personal victory.

Surprise is a most important factor in air fighting and a leader
should maneuver for position to achieve surprise before attacking, if possible. Surprise may be achieved by—

Attacking from directly out of sun,

Making use of the bank of haze. Aircraft approaching on the
same level are difficult to see if they attack from the side
remote from the sun. (A bomber, therefore, should try to
fly well above the haze level so as to render a concealed
approach by fighters less likely.)

In the evening or early morning by attacking from that part of
the sky which is darker,

By making good use of clouds or, in the case of fighters, by
making an intelligent estimate of where enemy aircraft is
likely to emerge.

When enemy aircraft is sighted in one direction, vigilance in
other directions must not be relaxed. More often than not other
supporting aircraft will be in the vicinity and to launch blithely

into the attack on the first enemy seen without a quick search for other enemy planes is a sure way to be shot out of the sky and never know what hit you.

III. SOME DO'S AND DON'TS

BEFORE taking off or landing, search the sky for enemy aircraft. It is at these moments your aircraft is most vulnerable.

If you hear gun fire, or see bullets hitting close to you or observe tracers going past *immediately* take evasive action—*then* look around. Don't try to look *before* starting to turn. It might be too late.

Develop a rubber neck. Keep the sky under constant surveillance.

Watch your tail.

Conserve ammunition.

Never fly or dive straight when being attacked by aircraft or anti-aircraft fire.

Fighters should endeavor not to close in on the enemy at too high a speed during the final stage of the approach or the burst of fire will be too short to be effective, or you may overshoot altogether.

Don't go into the middle of a V of enemy bombers. Attack them from the flank, and from both flanks simultaneously, where possible.

When you are going into the attack, don't give the enemy a chance at a deflection shot at you. As far as you can *keep your nose* on the enemy, and approach his blind spots as much as possible.

In attacking enemy bombers don't fire a long burst if enemy fighters are about; two seconds is long enough. Then break away quickly and look about to be sure no enemy fighter is after you. If all is clear you can take another crack at the bombers, if necessary.

Don't break away in a climbing turn. This gives an easy shot to the enemy rear gunner.

Don't leave your formation, if you can help it, unless ordered to do so.

Don't *ever* fly straight, especially if you are alone. Keep that rubber neck turning continuously and keep a lookout behind.

Don't let the enemy slip out of the sun to get you. In looking toward the sun place a finger or thumb before your eyes.

Don't waste ammunition by firing at long ranges.

IV. FORMATION PRINCIPLES

SIZE:

A large formation is more vulnerable to A. A. fire than a number of small formations.

The larger the formation the less maneuverable it becomes. However, it is more likely to subject attacking aircraft to a superior concentration of fire.

With a large formation there will be a tendency for a number of gunners to fire on a few enemy aircraft and to ignore others, and to waste ammunition. There is, therefore, a limit to the size of a formation to obtain economical fire concentration.

Aircraft which have blind sectors, or sectors of reduced fire power, need larger formations than those which have all around arcs of fire.

Small formations are less easily seen than large ones.

SHAPE:

Every pilot must be able *easily to see the* aircraft on which he is formating.

All aircraft in the formation must *keep station* on the leader, and as few as possible in *sequence*. Otherwise accumulated errors build up and the rearmost pilots have a very difficult task in maintaining proper position.

While being attacked, make it impossible to draw a straight line from the enemy aircraft line of approach through two or more aircraft of the formation. Otherwise the attackers may successfully *enfilade* the formation.

The length of the formation should be equal in all directions, where possible.

All aircraft in the formation, with possible exception of the leader to be equidistant from the enemy aircraft. Thus in defensive bomber formations every aircraft should be spread perpendicular to the enemy's line of approach.

Aircraft in formation should be *sufficiently far apart* to avoid one plane being hit by shots aimed at the other. At the same time they must be sufficiently close to provide maximum mutual support.

Formations disposed in depths create a large volume of slipstream turbulence which, when bombers are being attacked from rear, throws fighters off their line of sight.

The *ideal* defensive formation will differ with every method and direction of attack. Each formation must, therefore, possess sufficient flexibility to allow a quick alteration to some other formation.

The *disposition of aircraft* in formation will depend upon circumstances. For example, if attack on a defensive bomber formation is developing from above, aircraft in the formation should be stepped down—if the attack is from below the aircraft should be stepped up. If the attack is from the same level and developing from the beam aircraft should be stepped down (for it is *easier* for fighters to sweep a formation UPWARDS than DOWNWARDS. With aircraft on the nearer flank DOWN and on the outer flank UP.)

When encountering A. A. fire aircraft all sections should be far enough apart to avoid more than one aircraft being brought down by any one A. A. burst.

V. EVASION PRINCIPLES

ALWAYS turn *toward* a fighter. Thus you shorten his approach, and therefore make him turn more rapidly. Maybe he won't be able, aerodynamically, to turn fast enough and he may be forced to break away. DO NOT turn *away* from the direction of attack.

A straight dive will give enemy aircraft a "sitting shot." You actually appear as a stationary target in such a dive either at a target plane or away from the plane.

Never change from one turn to a reverse turn. *Wait* for a brief interval between attacks. Take a quick look about before launching successive attacks.

When hedge hopping, or flying low over the sea, fly an erratic course.

Clouds, except the smallest ones, afford one of the best means of avoiding enemy aircraft. When possible fly near the clouds, but if over areas covered by A. A. fire *do not* fly immediately below the cloud base, as A. A. can accurately determine the range from the cloud base.

Do not fly *straight* through a cloud when avoiding enemy aircraft. Alter course in the cloud to turn *towards* the enemy.

Aircraft flying above 20,000 feet are difficult to see from the ground.

Avoid layers of air in which white streamers form astern.

At night *do not* open throttle because this increases length of exhaust flame which can be seen at long distances.

Show no lights on your aircraft.

Searchlight beams without accompanying A. A. fire indicates presence of enemy fighters. Do everything possible to get out of the light.

To evade enemy fighters, fast bombers may be sent in advance of the striking force, to draw off enemy fighters. Also planes may be routed on dog-leg courses toward other important objectives with a view of deceiving the enemy as to the actual target.

EVADING SOUND LOCATORS

Searchlight and A. A. at night are directed by sound locators. (Radio aid is also said to be effective.) Sound locators may be avoided or deceived by one of the following means:

1. One aircraft to fly low, making a noise screen which will prevent aircraft flying high from being heard.

2. Gliding over the searchlight or A. A. belts in heights in excess of 6,000 feet where aircraft throttled back are inaudible.

3. Simultaneous raids on different or parallel courses at different heights will result in locators getting a false position.

4. Desynchronize engines. This is effective at least to inexperienced sound locator crews.

5. Most effective of all evasive measures are alterations in course, speed, and height.

Sound locator crews usually do not allow sufficiently for the lag in the time it takes the engine noise to reach them which results in searchlights and A. A. fire being below and behind. (Recently it seems German A. A. must be directed by radio-locators. Where radio-directed A. A. fire is encountered some of the foregoing suggestions, therefore will not apply.)

In seeking to avoid searchlights, *turn*. A climb or dive, *without turn* is ineffective.

VI. ANTI-AIRCRAFT EVASION

LONG RANGE A. A.

The A. A. gunner's greatest difficulty is finding the correct elevation. Consequently a change in height, as well as turning is the best method of evasion. Effective danger area of 3″ and 4.5″ shells is from 30 to 90 feet radius. The area behind and below the bursts is usually safe; therefore, it is best to fly below shell bursts rather than above them.

When within range of enemy A. A. it is imperative that course and altitude be altered continuously to avoid destructive hits.

Heavy A. A. fire is most accurate between 6,000 and 18,000 feet; therefore, if possible, fly above or below these heights.

The ideal target from A. A. point of view is a large formation in line astern. The most difficult formation for A. A. are small sections (of 2 or 3) flying line abreast, or shallow echelon, at different heights.

At night it has often proved effective to drop a flare, or other object, and then dive or climb on a turn. The enemy A.A. often concentrate on the flare or other object, and thus enable you to get-away.

SHORT RANGE A. A.

Short range A. A. is usually ineffective at heights above 5,000 feet. Therefore fly at greater heights, or else very low.

Attacks against defended areas should be made suddenly and *not repeated* for at least 5 or 10 minutes. Make a low and quick get-away without trying to maneuver to observe effect of your attack.

Low flying attacks should be made from the direction of the sun, or from clouds and by taking advantage of topographnical features.

If both short range and long range A. A. fire is expected the best compromise is probably to fly at about 5,000 feet, at ground level, or above 18,000 feet.

SPECIFICATIONS

SILHOUETTES BY JACK RIGNEY

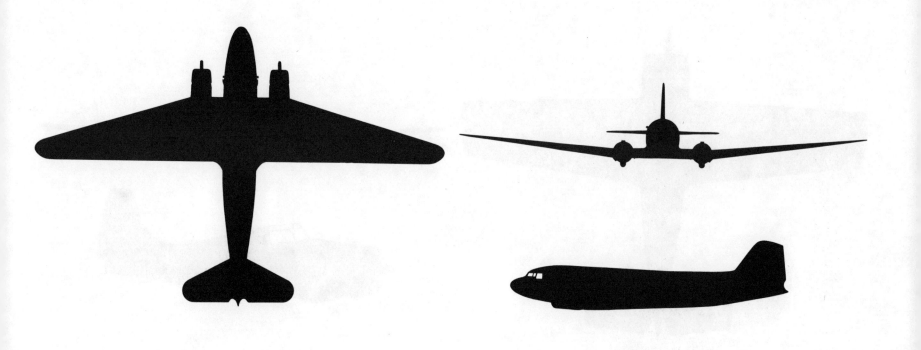

WING SPAN:	95 feet
LENGTH:	64 feet, 6 inches
HEIGHT:	16 feet, 11 inches
WING AREA:	987 square feet
POWER:	Two Pratt & Whitney R-1830s/1,200 h.p. each
WEIGHT:	Empty: 17,900 pounds
	Loaded: 26,900 pounds
CRUISING SPEED:	180 m.p.h.
RANGE:	1,300 miles

(GRUMMAN) GENERAL MOTORS FM-2 "WILDCAT" (XF4F-8)

WING SPAN:	38 feet
LENGTH:	28 feet, 11 inches
HEIGHT:	11 feet, 5 inches
WING AREA:	260 square feet
POWER:	One Wright R-1820-56/1,350 h.p.
WEIGHT:	Empty: 5,448 pounds
	Loaded: 8,271 pounds
MAXIMUM SPEED:	332 m.p.h.
SERVICE CEILING:	34,700 feet
RANGE:	1,310 miles

Author's note: The CAF "Wildcat" is a version of the Grumman XF4F-8 produced by the General Motors Eastern Aircraft Division.

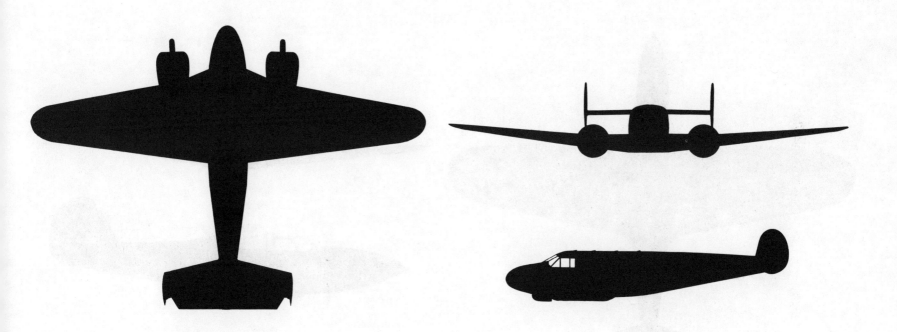

WING SPAN:	47 feet, 8 inches
LENGTH:	34 feet, 3 inches
HEIGHT:	9 feet, 5 inches
WING AREA:	374 square feet
POWER:	Two Pratt & Whitney Wasp-Junior engines/ 450 h.p. each
WEIGHT:	Empty: 5,025 pounds
	Loaded: 7,500 pounds
MAXIMUM SPEED:	220 m.p.h.
SERVICE CEILING:	27,000 feet
RANGE:	1,000 miles

BELL P-39Q "AIRACOBRA"

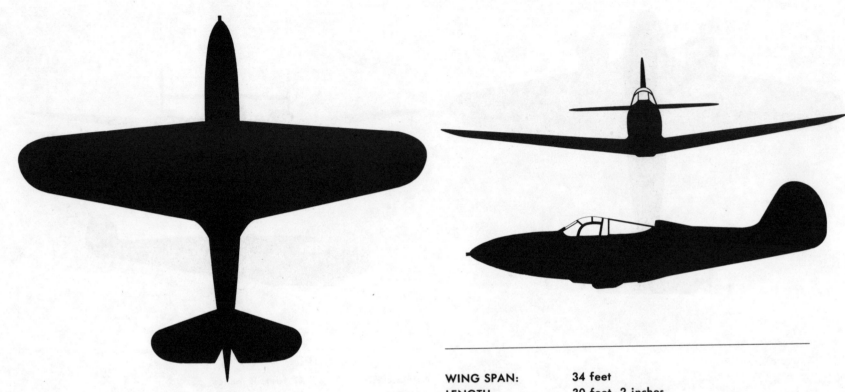

WING SPAN:	34 feet
LENGTH:	30 feet, 2 inches
HEIGHT:	12 feet, 5 inches
WING AREA:	213 square feet
POWER:	One Allison V-1710-85/1,420 h.p.
WEIGHT	Empty: 5,645 pounds
	Loaded: 8,300 pounds
MAXIMUM SPEED:	385 m.p.h.
SERVICE CEILING:	35,000 feet
RANGE:	1,250 miles

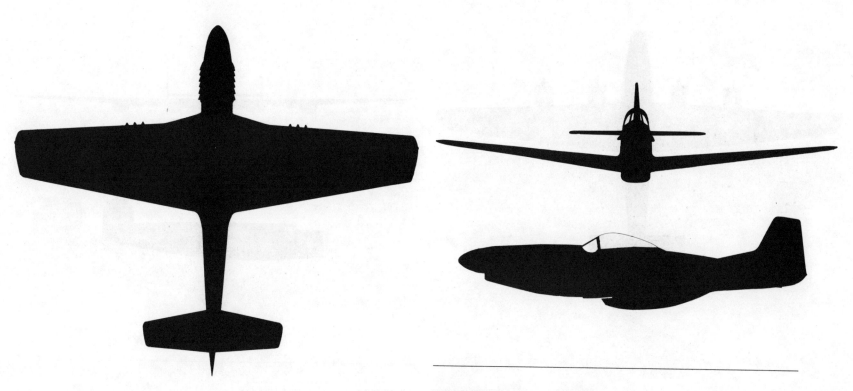

WING SPAN:	37 feet
LENGTH:	32 feet, 3 inches
HEIGHT:	13 feet, 8 inches
WING AREA:	233 square feet
POWER:	One Packard V-1650-7/1,720 h.p.
WEIGHT:	Empty: 7,125 pounds
	Loaded: 11,600 pounds
MAXIMUM SPEED:	437 m.p.h.
SERVICE CEILING:	41,900 feet
RANGE:	2,300 miles

CONSOLIDATED LB-30 "LIBERATOR II" (B-24)

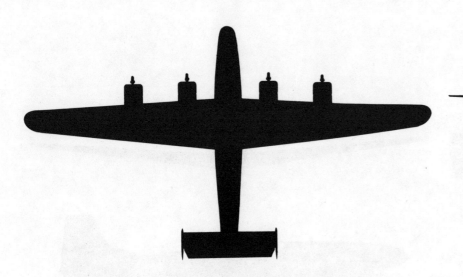

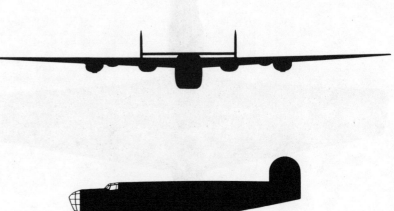

WING SPAN:	110 feet
LENGTH:	67 feet, 2 inches
HEIGHT:	18 feet
WING AREA:	1,048 square feet
POWER:	Four Pratt & Whitney R-1830-65s/1,200 h.p. each
WEIGHT:	Empty: 36,500 pounds
	Loaded: 65,000 pounds
MAXIMUM SPEED:	290 m.p.h.
SERVICE CEILING:	28,000 feet
RANGE:	3,700 miles

Author's note: The CAF "Liberator" is a version built in San Diego for the Royal Air Force and delivered under the designation LB-30 (Liberator built to British specifications).

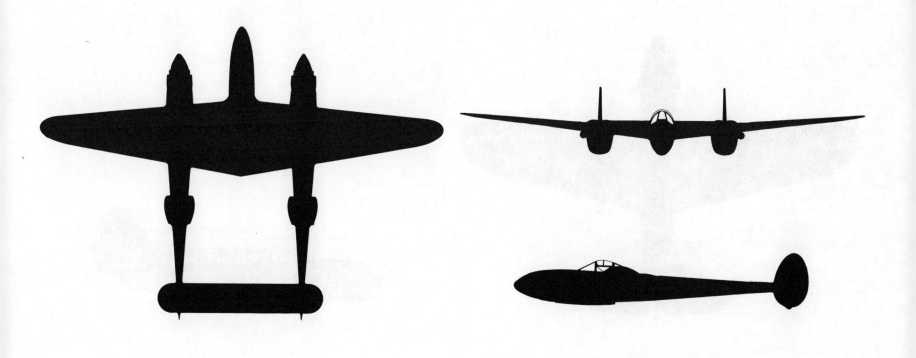

WING SPAN:	52 feet
LENGTH:	37 feet, 10 inches
HEIGHT:	9 feet, 10 inches
WING AREA:	327.5 square feet
POWER:	Two Allison V-1710-111s/1,600 h.p. each
WEIGHT:	Empty: 12,800 pounds
	Loaded: 21,600 pounds
MAXIMUM SPEED:	414 m.p.h.
SERVICE CEILING:	44,000 feet
RANGE:	2,600 miles

Author's note: The CAF P-38 (as photographed) is a P-38L with cowling
modifications.

CURTISS SB2C-5 "HELLDIVER"

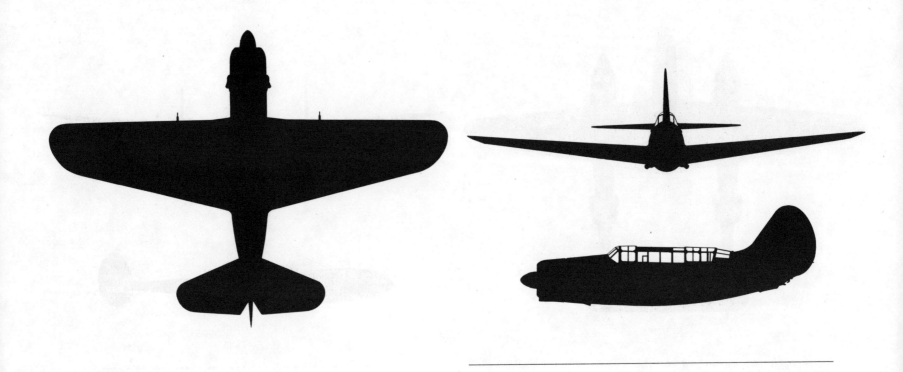

WING SPAN:	49 feet, 9 inches
LENGTH:	36 feet, 8 inches
HEIGHT:	13 feet, 2 inches
WING AREA:	422 square feet
POWER:	One Wright R-2600-20/1,900 h.p.
WEIGHT:	Empty: 10,589 pounds
	Loaded: 16,287 pounds
MAXIMUM SPEED:	290 m.p.h.
SERVICE CEILING:	27,600 feet
RANGE:	1,324 miles

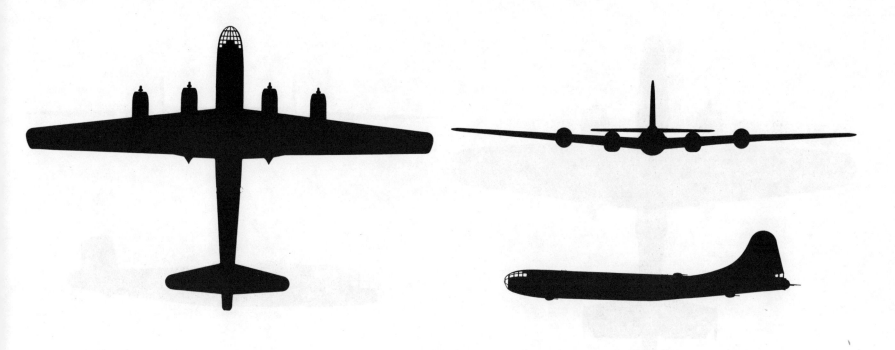

WING SPAN:	141 feet, 3 inches
LENGTH:	99 feet
HEIGHT:	29 feet, 7 inches
WING AREA:	1,736 square feet
POWER:	Four R-3350-57s/2,500 h.p. each
WEIGHT:	Empty: 72,208 pounds
	Loaded: 140,000 pounds
MAXIMUM SPEED:	399 m.p.h.
SERVICE CEILING:	23,950 feet
RANGE:	5,418 miles

NORTH AMERICAN TB-25N "MITCHELL" (B-25J)

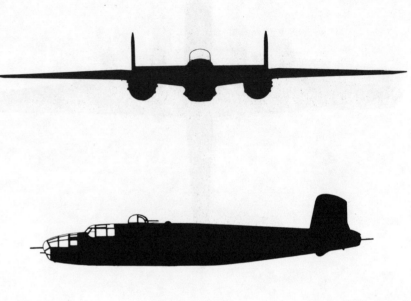

WING SPAN:	67 feet, 7 inches
LENGTH:	52 feet, 11 inches
HEIGHT:	16 feet, 4 inches
WING AREA:	610 square feet
POWER:	Two Wright R-2600-29/1,700 h.p. each
WEIGHT:	Empty: 19,480 pounds
	Loaded: 35,000 pounds
MAXIMUM SPEED:	272 m.p.h.
SERVICE CEILING:	24,200 feet
RANGE:	1,350 miles

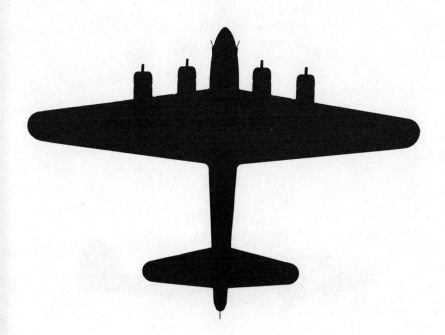

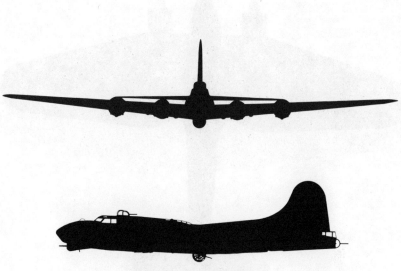

WING SPAN:	103 feet, 9 inches
LENGTH:	74 feet, 4 inches
HEIGHT:	19 feet, 1 inch
WING AREA:	1,420 square feet
POWER:	Four Wright R-1820-97s/1,200 h.p. each
WEIGHT:	Empty: 36,135 pounds
	Loaded: 65,500 pounds
MAXIMUM SPEED:	287 m.p.h.
SERVICE CEILING:	35,600 feet
RANGE:	3,400 miles

HEINKEL He 111

WING SPAN:	74 feet, 1½ inches
LENGTH:	54 feet, 5½ inches
HEIGHT:	13 feet, 9 inches
WING AREA:	942 square feet
POWER:	Two Junkers Jumo 211F-2s/1,340 h.p. each
WEIGHT:	Empty: 14,400 pounds
	Loaded: 27,400 pounds
MAXIMUM SPEED:	258 m.p.h.
SERVICE CEILING:	25,500 feet
RANGE:	1,740 miles

Author's note: The CAF He 111 was produced in Spain under license of the Heinkel factory by Construcciónes Aeronauticas S.A.

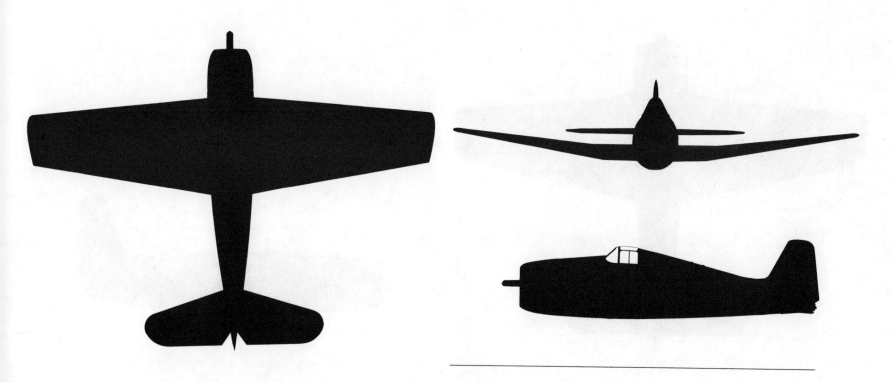

WING SPAN:	42 feet, 10 inches
LENGTH:	33 feet, 7 inches
HEIGHT:	13 feet, 1 inch
WING AREA:	334 square feet
POWER:	One Pratt & Whitney R-2800-10W/2,000 h.p.
WEIGHT:	Empty: 9,238 pounds
	Loaded: 15,413 pounds
MAXIMUM SPEED:	380 m.p.h.
SERVICE CEILING:	37,300 feet
RANGE:	1,355 miles

GRUMMAN F8F-2 "BEARCAT"

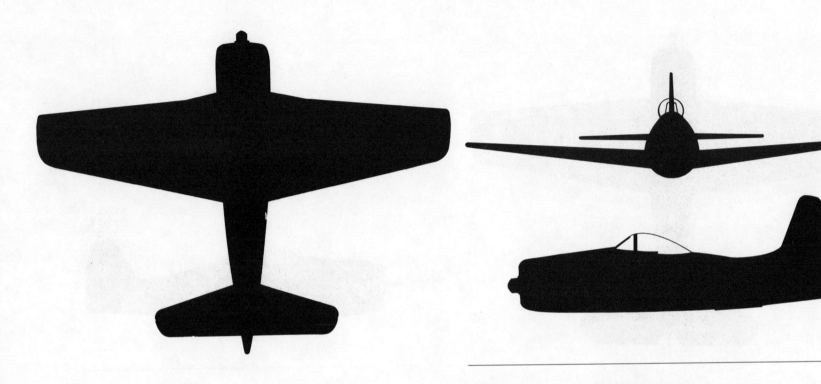

WING SPAN:	35 feet, 6 inches
LENGTH:	27 feet, 8 inches
HEIGHT:	12 feet, 2 inches
WING AREA:	244 square feet
POWER:	One Pratt & Whitney R-2800-34W/2,300 h.p.
WEIGHT:	Empty: 7,690 pounds
	Loaded: 13,494 pounds
MAXIMUM SPEED:	447 m.p.h.
SERVICE CEILING:	40,700 feet
RANGE:	1,435 miles

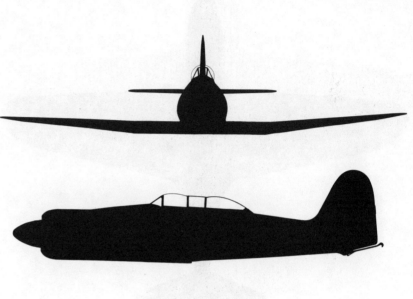

WING SPAN:	38 feet, 4¾ inches
LENGTH:	34 feet, 7 inches
WING AREA:	280 square feet
POWER:	One Bristol Centaurus 18/2,480 h.p.
WEIGHT:	Empty: 8,700 pounds
	Loaded: 11,930 pounds
MAXIMUM SPEED:	445 m.p.h.
SERVICE CEILING:	35,600 feet
RANGE:	1,310 miles

CURTISS P-40N "WARHAWK"

WING SPAN:	37 feet, 4 inches
LENGTH:	33 feet, 4 inches
HEIGHT:	12 feet, 4 inches
WING AREA:	236 square feet
POWER:	One Allison V-1710-81/1,360 h.p.
WEIGHT:	Empty: 6,000 pounds
	Loaded: 8,850 pounds
MAXIMUM SPEED:	378 m.p.h.
SERVICE CEILING:	38,000 feet
RANGE:	1,400 miles

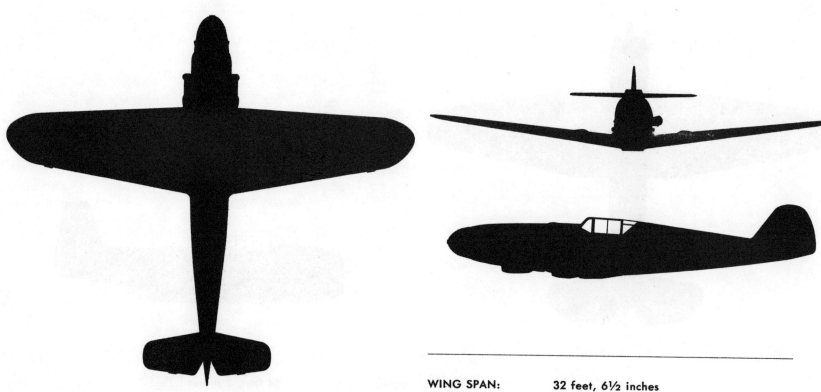

WING SPAN:	32 feet, 6½ inches
LENGTH:	29 feet, 4 inches
HEIGHT:	12 feet
WING AREA:	173 square feet
POWER:	One Daimler-Benz DB605ASCM/DCM/2,000 h.p.
WEIGHT:	Loaded: 7,438 pounds
MAXIMUM SPEED:	377 m.p.h.
SERVICE CEILING:	41,000 feet
RANGE:	355 miles

Author's note: The CAF Messerschmitts are variants produced under license in Spain by Hispano Aviación with German tooling.

(GRUMMAN) GENERAL MOTORS TBM-1C "AVENGER"

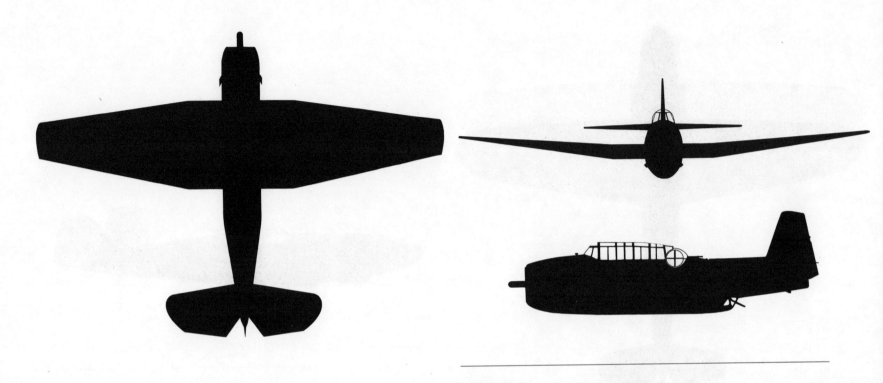

WING SPAN:	54 feet, 2 inches
LENGTH:	40 feet
HEIGHT:	16 feet, 5 inches
WING AREA:	490 square feet
POWER:	One Wright R-2600-8/1,700 h.p.
WEIGHT:	Empty: 10,555 pounds
	Loaded: 17,364 pounds
MAXIMUM SPEED:	257 m.p.h.
SERVICE CEILING:	21,400 feet
RANGE:	2,335 miles

Author's note: The CAF "Avenger" is a TBM manufactured by the General Motors Eastern Aircraft Division under Grumman license.

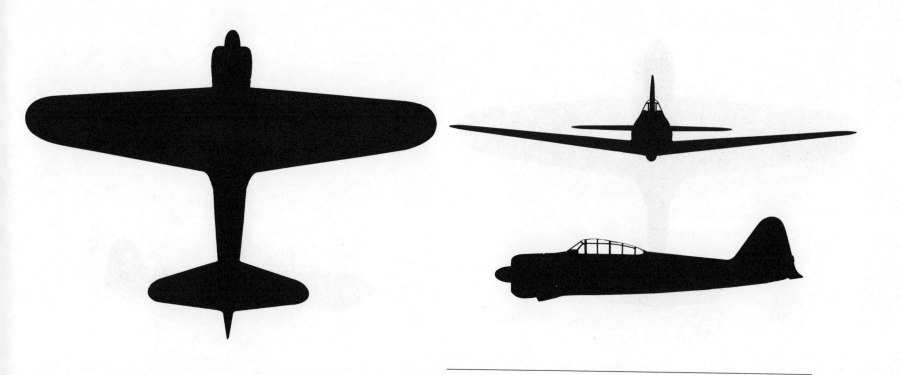

WING SPAN:	36 feet, 1 inch
LENGTH:	29 feet, 9 inches
HEIGHT:	9 feet, 2 inches
WING AREA:	229 square feet
POWER:	One Nakajima NK1P Sakae 31/1,210 h.p.
WEIGHT:	Empty: 3,920 pounds
	Loaded: 6,508 pounds
MAXIMUM SPEED:	346 m.p.h.
SERVICE CEILING:	35,100 feet
RANGE:	1,130 miles

Author's note: The CAF "Zeros" are replicas built by Twentieth Century-Fox for the motion picture *Tora! Tora! Tora!*

NAKAJIMA B5N "KATE"

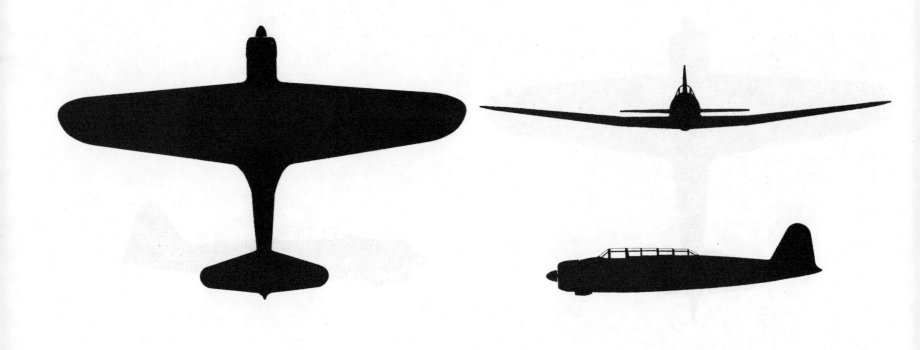

WING SPAN:	50 feet, 11 inches
LENGTH:	33 feet, 10 inches
HEIGHT:	12 feet, 2 inches
WING AREA:	412 square feet
POWER:	One Sakae II/1,000 h.p.
WEIGHT:	Empty: 4,830 pounds
	Loaded: 8,360 pounds
MAXIMUM SPEED:	235 m.p.h.
SERVICE CEILING:	25,200 feet
RANGE:	1,238 miles

Author's note: The CAF "Kate" is a replica built by Twentieth Century-Fox
for the motion picture *Tora! Tora! Tora!*

Typefaces: Spartan and Times Roman set by Waldman Graphics, Philadelphia

Color Separations: Offset Separations Corporation, Turin, Italy

Color Insert Printing: Pearl, Pressman, Liberty Printers, Philadelphia

Color Insert Paper: Lustro Offset Enamel Gloss from S. D. Warren

Text Printing and Binding: The Book Press, Brattleboro, Vermont

Design: Robert Reed

Editorial Production: Jill Gutelle

Production: Karen Gillis